Published by Creative Education
P.O. Box 227, Mankato, Minnesota 56002
Creative Education is an imprint of The Creative Company
www.thecreativecompany.us

Design and Production by The Design Lab
Printed in the United States of America

Photographs by Corbis (Dean Conger, Historical Picture Archive, Jutta Klee, Joe McDonald, Reuters, Joseph Sohm/Visions of America, Spaceborne Imaging Radar-C/X-Band Synthetic Aperture Radar/ NASA, James Sparshatt, Keren Su), iStockphoto (George Clerk, CPW, Ke Wang, Xin Zhu)

Library of Congress Cataloging-in-Publication Data
Riggs, Kate.
Great Wall of China / by Kate Riggs.
p. cm. — (Places of old)
Includes index.
ISBN 978-1-58341-708-9
1. Great Wall of China (China)—Juvenile literature. I. Title.
DS793.G67.R54 2009   951—dc22   2007051892

First edition

2 4 6 8 9 7 5 3 1

GREAT WALL OF CHINA

by Kate Riggs

CREATIVE EDUCATION

THE GREAT WALL OF CHINA is a long, stone wall. It is in China. It is about 4,000

miles (6,440 km) long! Some parts of it are 26 feet (8 m) high.

The main Great Wall branches off to form other walls

Qin Shi Huang (*chin sure hwong*) was the first emperor of China. He had workers start building the Great Wall about 2,200 years ago. But most of that wall fell apart. About 400 years ago, people called the Ming built the wall people can see today.

Millions of handmade bricks make up the Great Wall

Soldiers stood on tall watchtowers along the wall

The Great Wall of China is nicknamed the "Sleeping Dragon" because of its long, snakelike shape.

To build the wall, the Ming made bricks out of mud. They baked them in ovens called kilns. Then they built towers and connected the wall to the towers. They also used stone to make the wall stronger.

The Ming leaders ruled China for more than 275 years and wanted to keep people called Mongols out.

Making bricks out of mud is a messy process

More than one million Ming soldiers guarded the wall

Qin Shi Huang built the Great Wall to protect his people from invaders. The Ming rebuilt the wall to protect themselves, too.

The wall marked the northern borders of China long ago

The wall that the Ming built was strong. The Ming built drains into the wall so that rain would run off. Then the water would not get inside the wall and make it fall apart.

The wall winds across many hills in northeastern China

The clay, or terracotta, soldiers look like real people

Qin Shi Huang had an army of life-sized clay soldiers built for his tomb (TOOM). He died in 210 B.C.

It takes a lot of people to restore parts of the wall

The Great Wall is not all one piece anymore. Some parts are very old and are falling apart. Many of the broken parts are being restored. People are rebuilding the wall like the Ming did.

Some older parts of the Great Wall of China are underneath rivers now.

China did not always let people from other countries come see the Great Wall. But millions of people from around the world have visited it every year since the 1970s.

To people near Earth in outer space, the Great Wall does not look like a wall.

People visiting China carry maps to know where to go

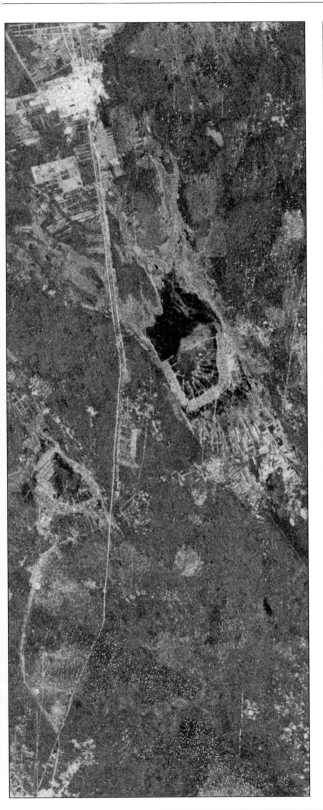

From space, the Great Wall looks like a long line

People can climb and walk on parts of the Great Wall

The best times of year to visit the Great Wall are spring and early fall. Then it is warmer during the day. Winters can get very cold in China. People do not want to be walking on the wall then.

There are many steps all over the Great Wall. Some steps are very steep*!*

The Great Wall is the longest human-made structure in the world. It does not keep people

About 10 million people visit the wall each year

out of China anymore, though.
Now, it welcomes people in!

Some soldiers probably rode horses to patrol the wall

glossary

emperor
a ruler who controls his kingdom, which is called
an empire

invaders
people who enter land that is not theirs and try to
take it away from people who live there

restored
brought back to the way it used to be

steep
rising or falling sharply

read more about it

Fisher, Leonard Everett. *The Great Wall of China.* New York: Aladdin Paperbacks/Simon & Schuster, 1995.

Morley, Jacqueline, and David Salariya. *You Wouldn't Want to Work on the Great Wall of China! Defenses You'd Rather Not Build.* New York: Franklin Watts, 2006.

index